Dinosaur Babies

by Leonie Bennett

Consultant: Dougal Dixon

Copyright © **ticktock Entertainment Ltd 2007**
First published in Great Britain in 2007 by **ticktock Media Ltd.,**
Unit 2, Orchard Business Centre, North Farm Road, Tunbridge Wells, Kent TN2 3XF

We would like to thank: Shirley Bickler and Suzanne Baker

ISBN 978 1 84696 607 1
Printed in China

Picture credits
t=top, b=bottom, c=centre, l-left, r=right, OFC= outside front cover
Simon Mendez: 4c, 8-9, 16; Philip Hood: 1, 4cr, 5l, 5r, 7, 8l, 11b, 11tr, 13b, 17, 19, 22tl, 22br; Shutterstock: 6c, 6b; Luis Rey: 10l, 20-21; John Alston: 12, 21t; Corbis: 13tr; Pulsar EStudio: 14-15, 23c.

CONTENTS

Dinosaur eggs

Dinosaurs laid eggs.

Some dinosaur eggs were oval.

Troodon eggs were oval.

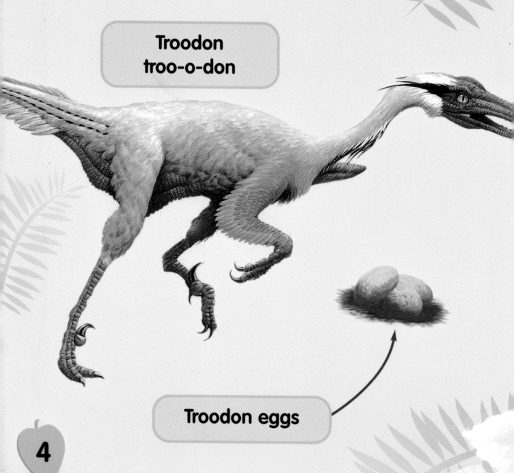

Troodon
troo-o-don

Troodon eggs

4

Therizinosaur
ther-ee-zine-o-sor

Some dinosaur
eggs were round.

This dinosaur's eggs
were round.

Therizinosaur
egg

5

How big were dinosaur eggs?

Some eggs were bigger
than a football.

Some eggs were
smaller than a golf ball.

The biggest dinosaur egg we know belongs to this dinosaur. It was about 30 centimetres long.

Hypselosaurus
hip-sel-o-sor-us

7

Where did dinosaurs lay their eggs?

Some dinosaurs laid their eggs in nests.

The nests were made of earth.

They were on the ground.

Eggs

Some animals lived in the sea.

This one came to land to lay its eggs.
It dug a hole and laid its eggs in it.

Plesiosaur
pless-ee-o-sor

Keeping the eggs warm

This dinosaur is sitting on its nest.

It is keeping its eggs warm.

Oviraptor
ov-ee-rap-tor

Big dinosaurs
did not sit on
their eggs.
They might
break them!

Big dinosaurs hid their eggs in a pile of
leaves. The leaves kept the eggs
safe and warm.

How big were dinosaur babies?

Apatosaurus was one of the biggest dinosaurs. A baby Apatosaurus was as big as a cat.

Apatosaurus
a-pat-o-sor-us

baby   adult

The baby grew very fast. At 15 years old it was almost as big as an adult.

This is a skeleton of a baby dinosaur.

It is a baby Mussaurus.

**Mussaurus
moo-sor-us**

Looking after the babies

Some dinosaurs looked after their babies.

They kept them safe from danger.

Tyrannosaurus rex
tie-ran-o-sor-us rex

This dinosaur mother is fighting a meat-eater.

The meat-eater wants to eat her baby.

Triceratops
try-serra-tops

What did dinosaur babies eat?

Some dinosaurs were plant-eaters.

Their babies ate leaves and twigs.

They had to learn to find the plants they liked.

Some dinosaurs were meat-eaters.

Their babies had to learn to hunt.

Special dinosaur mothers

Look at the Maiasaura. Its name means 'good mother lizard'.

It looked after its babies.

This dinosaur mother chewed the leaves of plants to make them soft. Then she gave them to her babies.

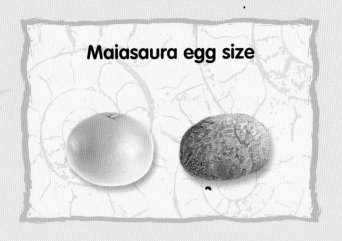

Maiasaura egg size

Maiasaura eggs were as big as grapefruits.

Maiasaura
my-a-sor-a

Icthyosaurus

This dinosaur lived in the sea.

It did not lay eggs.

It did not make a nest.

This dinosaur's babies were born alive.

They were born underwater.

Icthyosaurus
ick-thee-o-sor-us

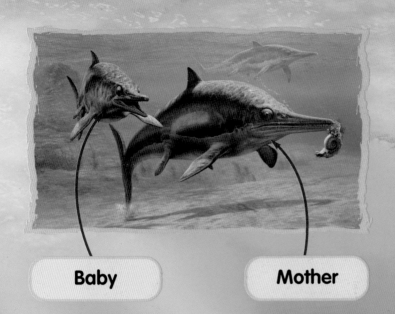

Baby

Mother

Thinking and talking about dinosaurs

Some dinosaur eggs were oval.

Yes or no?

Big dinosaurs sat on their eggs.

Yes or no?

Dinosaurs made
their nests
in trees.

Yes or no?

Triceratops did
not look after
its babies.

Yes or no?

Would you like to
look after a
dinosaur baby?

r why not?

23

Activities

What did you think of this book?

 Brilliant **Good**  **OK**

Which page did you like best? Why?

• • • • • • • • • • • • • •

Make a sentence with these words:

eggs • dinosaur • were • Some • round.

• • • • • • • • • • • • • •

Draw a picture of a baby dinosaur.
What kind of dinosaur is it?

• • • • • • • • • • • • • •

Who is the author of this book?
Have you read *Dinosaur Fossils*
by the same author?